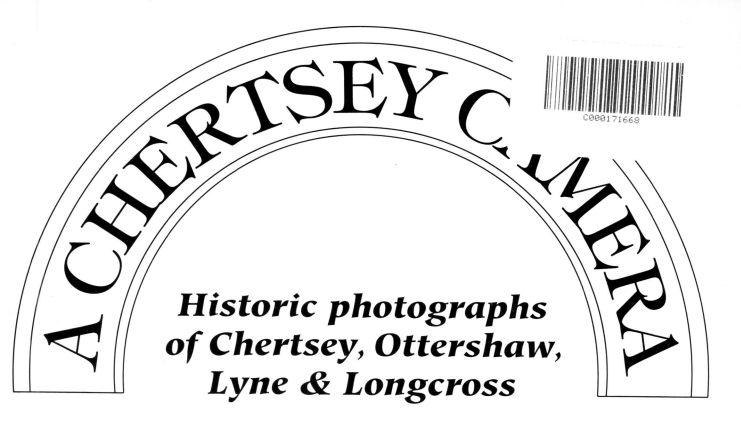

A CHERTSEY CAMERA

Historic photographs of Chertsey, Ottershaw, Lyne & Longcross

D. M. & J. L. BARKER

In memory of Mary Daniel, 11th Jan. 1926 – 21st July 1992, the first Honorary Curator of Chertsey Museum, to whom the historians of Chertsey owe so much.

Introduction

In the 12 years since the publication of Mr. H.J.M. Stratton's original photographic collection, a great deal of new material has come to light. Some of this, together with relevant historical notes, is presented here.

Once again it is necessary to acknowledge the skills of previous generations of photographers, whose work is now receiving due recognition. Many aspects of life in this part of the present Borough of Runnymede were photographed during the heyday of the picture postcard; the decade before the First World War. We are also pleased to include one of the earliest surviving photographs of an archaeological excavation and a picture of the construction of the Lyne railway bridge. The influence of Chertsey Abbey and the motorway network are thus jointly recognised.

The Chertsey area, although comparatively fortunate in retaining a significant number of period buildings, has nevertheless suffered losses and alterations. For this reason the photographic record, like no other medium, permits the permanent visualisation of many of these scenes. To this end we have attempted to arrange the contents in a topographical sequence, starting at the Thames and ending on the borders of Addlestone at Spratts Lane. Some of this material may be familiar to long-established residents, although we believe the majority of the photographs are reproduced here for the first time.

Although the area covered exhibits great contrasts both in wealth and topography, its very diversity gives Chertsey, Ottershaw, Lyne and Longcross their own very distinctive character. We hope this selection will illustrate some of these contrasts, as captured by the camera. We also hope that the collection will add to the appreciation of all aspects of local history fostered by various eminent local historians, amenity groups, and above all by Chertsey Museum, with its key role in preserving the material and photographic heritage of the area.

December 1992

Front Cover

Chertsey's last town crier, the redoubtable Mrs. Mary Ann Blaker, who took over from her husband in 1914 and refused to give up the job on his return from the war. She continued until her death aged 71 in 1940. The uniform, originally made by Albert Crewdson for her father-in-law, Henry Blaker, in 1905, was trimmed with gold braid and consisted of a blue coat and matching waistcoat, both lined with scarlet, black tricorn hat, white scarf, and black kid shoes with silver buckles. The original breeches, worn with yellow stockings, were replaced by a black skirt. The photograph is by William Bates & Son of Eastworth Road, who were active from at least 1882 to c. 1927.

Chertsey Lock, 1913

Pictured in the newly-rebuilt lock in July 1913 are some of the diverse craft which were a familiar sight on this stretch of the river. The custom of "Swan Upping", a census of the swan population on the Thames belonging to the Crown and the Vintners, and Dyers, Companies of the City of London, was carried out during the third week in July. A pleasure launch, the "Antrim", is complemented by the working barge of Emmanuel Smith of Brentford. At this time the lock keeper was James Basson, who came from Marsh Lock on the Thames.

A Pleasure Launch at Chertsey Lock c. 1895

At this period, steam launches provided a very popular forerunner of the modern coach trip, often used for staff outings. Photographers would wait by the locks to photograph such parties on the outward journey, and sell prints to the passengers on their way home. This example by William Bates probably shows the 72-ft. "Windsor Castle", built by James Taylor in 1892 and licensed to carry 150. She was renamed "Balmoral" in 1904 and later sold to J. T. Mears of Richmond, eventually being broken up in 1947. Note the piano for on-board entertainment! James Taylor had started a steam saw mills at Bridge Wharf in 1850, and opened his boatyard there in 1891 with his son-in-law, W. B. Bates, as manager. The firm later became Taylor & Bates and, by 1938, W. Bates & Son. Taylor was particularly noted for his houseboats. On the far bank can be seen the rival boatyard of Tom Taylor (no relation).

The Great Frost, 1890-91

Local people are here captured by William Bates "walking on the water" by Chertsey Lock and Weir in what was then believed to be the coldest winter for 150 years. The "Surrey News" in December 1890 reported skating in the area, a soup kitchen organised by Mrs. W. A. Herring and a proposal to set up a labour yard for the "deserving poor". An earlier frost in February 1855 was recalled by a local resident, who remembered football and dancing taking place under the central arch of Chertsey Bridge.

DesVignes Torpedo Boat, Chertsey Meads, c. 1883

George Francis Gabriel DesVignes began building his first steam launch, the "Calypso", in his family's garden at Tulse Hill, South London, in 1864 at the age of 16, and completed it in 1867. In 1871-2 he rented a yard adjacent to James Taylor's boatyard, where he built some of the finest steam launches ever made. He later advertised that he had built boats for the British, French, Russian, Greek and Peruvian Governments. A torpedo boat, pictured by William Bates on the river at Chertsey Meads, was one of several built for the Imperial Ottoman Navy. This one, most likely the largest, was 130 ft. long and capable of just over 23 knots, with engines of 1,240 indicated horse power. In 1886 he built two steam submarines, "Abdul Hamid" and "Abdul Medjid", for the Turks, but they never saw active service. DesVignes was unfortunately not a good businessman and became bankrupt in 1887, later becoming Works Manager to the Kingdon Yacht, Launch & Engineering Co. Ltd. of Teddington when they took over his business there in April 1892.

DesVignes Steam Engine c. 1880s

Chertsey has a long and continuing tradition of high-quality engineering, and George DesVignes utilised this in his yard by the Thames. Photographed here by William Bates outside DesVignes' works is an example of one of the steam engines for which he was so famous. This example has a single cylinder with a slide valve, a heavily ribbed valve chest cover and Stephenson's link reversing gear. Each component was as strongly and lightly constructed as possible, without using an ounce more metal than was necessary. In contrast with the heavy cast iron frames made by most of his contemporaries, DesVignes has used two slender turned steel columns.

Anglers at "The Cricketers", 1914

Members of the Amalgamated Thameside Angling Association are shown here arriving at "The Cricketers", Bridge Road, for a competition on 13th September 1914 . The bearded man in the centre is their President, H. Warren, Esq. "The Cricketers" had been the home of the Chertsey Angling Society from at least 1895, and at this time Bert Botting (a local grocer and wine merchant) was their Hon. Sec . At the same time the Chertsey Town Angling Association, whose members fished the Abbey River, was operating from "The Swan" in Windsor Street. "The Cricketers" had presumably been frequented by anglers for a long time, as a letter of c. 1825-30 mentions "an immense fish that is painted on the wall of the entrance passage" in the old building. The inn, originally called "The Walnut Tree", was in existence in the early 18th century, but was rebuilt c. 1880. It closed in 1990.

Bridge Road c. 1935

The Bridge Hotel opened c. 1870 on a site formerly occupied by a wharf. The Attfield family, who ran the wharf for several generations, built the early 18th century house at 77 Bridge Road, seen beyond the hotel. By the mid-19th century it had become a boys' boarding school. The covered walkway visible between the two buildings belonged to the Lewis Tea Cottage, run by Mrs. Grace Potter. C. Brown had recently opened the Bridge Garage at no. 102, opposite.

Chertsey Sports, 1912

Annual sports and pony races took place in a field
called The Hollows on the corner of Bridge Road
and Willow Walk. The August Bank Holiday events
continued here until 1934, and then transferred to
Abbey Chase. Here, Henry Bishop of Englefield
Green is seen riding "Cranbourne Lass", winner of
the Abbey Cup for ponies under 14.2 hands. The
trophy was a gift from Chertsey solicitor Henry
Paine.

Local Labourers, 1861

Following the important discoveries of 1855,
further work on the Abbey site was carried out by
the new tenant of the land, Sam Angell, in 1861.
The actual task of excavation was carried out by
local labour, the gentlemen archaeologists of the
time directing their work. As well as photographs
of the mediaeval features revealed during the
work, this one of a group of Chertsey men was
also taken. The man in the centre is thought to be
Henry Mason, aged 43, who lived in Willow Walk,
and whose occupation was agricultural labourer.
Sam Angell recorded that at one stage of the
excavation he was compelled to wait for the
completion of the wheat harvest before he could
carry on. No doubt the importance of getting crops
in outweighed the temporary pick and shovel work
for the local workers. Henry Mason is seen wearing
a typical Surrey round smock, a distinct type of the
common protective garment of the countryman.
Its use was already beginning to die out in the face
of cheap mass-produced clothing and the
introduction of powered machinery, which made
such garments dangerous to wear.

Wesleyan Methodist Church, London Street, 1898

Chertsey's first Methodist Chapel stood in White Hart Lane in the early 19th century. Work on the new church commenced in April 1863 and was completed by 23rd October the same year. The building work was financed by Mr. Joshua Richards of Addlestone, who had offered £500 for that purpose in 1860. Rooms for a Sunday school costing £310 were opened in 1867. Further work to the interior of the church was carried out in 1896, including the fitting of stained glass. As part of the drive to produce war weapons during the Second World War the iron railings seen in the photograph were removed. The building closed for worship at the end of May 1982 and Chertsey's Methodist congregation now share the parish church of St. Peter's. Demolition of the Methodist Church in 1986-87 took longer than its building!

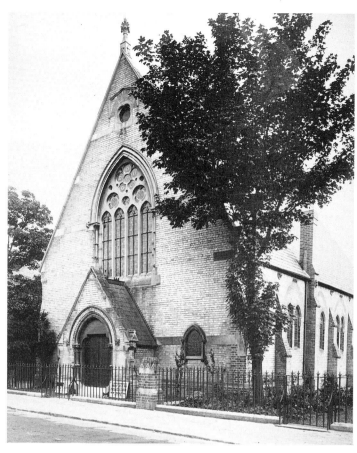

W. Beach, Blacksmith, 50 London Street c. 1900

Blacksmith's Lane has been the location of a series of eponymous craftsmen from at least the mid-19th century. A succession of blacksmiths and farriers had occupied the forge here used by William Beach; pictured on the left with Jim Saunders beside him. William Beach had arrived c. 1900, but in 1905 the premises were being used by the Melrose Motor Works, with Walter Taylor as Engineer. The motor works moved to 79 Guildford Street by 1910, and the forge was taken over by William Abbis, who moved to Addlestone soon afterwards. Other smiths, including Harry Thompson, later occupied the site before it eventually became the St. John Ambulance garage. The site has now (1992) reverted to ironworking.

The Xtra, 1922

One of many small cars produced briefly in the 1920s was the Xtra cyclecar, built at 45-47 London Street by Xtra Cars Ltd. The little single-seater 3-wheeled car had a beechwood body, motorcycle wheels, a 2¾ hp single-cylinder Villiers engine, 2-speed transmission and acetylene lamps. Fuel consumption was 80 mpg and it could reach a speed of well over 30 mph. The well-upholstered seat and unusual suspension system with no front axle gave a comfortable ride, but it is said that the vehicle tended to tip over if corners were taken too fast! The Xtra first appeared at the December 1921 Motor Cycle Show, retailing at 95 guineas. It was not a great success and production ceased in 1924.

A Chertsey Milkman, 1928

Thomas Henry Richards' "Fern Dairy" operated from 43 London Street between 1926 and the beginning of the Second World War. The site had previously been occupied by members of the Vincent family as cowkeepers and dairymen from c. 1845. Although glass milk bottles were available, many small dairies continued the more picturesque, though less hygenic, method of delivering pint and half-pint measures into customers' own containers. Here, milkman George Ernest Winder is seen on his rounds with a smart handcart.

P. J. Percey's Shop, 1911

Percy James Percey, carpenter & undertaker, set up shop at 41 London Street around 1905, moving across the road to number 42 about 20 years later, after which these premises became a hotel. B.A. Gorrad photographed him with his family outside the shop during the Coronation festivities of 1911. Behind the shop can be seen buildings associated with the maltings which had operated here in the 19th century.

London Street Looking East c. 1931

A quiet London Street, photographed around 1931, contained many long-established local businesses. Although architecturally little altered, much change of use has occurred in the succeeding 60 years. Seen on the right at no. 24 was Mrs. Charlotte Hume's confectioners (opened by 1923). Next door were the premises of Albert Blaker, bootmaker and sometime Chertsey Town Crier. The Compasses public house, which closed in the early 1960s, was said to have been an inn since the 17th century and was certainly so by 1785. It was known as The Duke's Head in 1814, but appears to have ceased trading for some years in the 1820s. No. 30, Cambridge House, a fine Italianate style building of mid-19th century date, was the home of the medical practice of Messrs. Milsome, Harmens and Taylor. Beyond this, John Hollick's family rope and twine business also supplied tents, marquees and tarpaulins, all made on the premises.

London Street From Windsor Street c. 1920

The premises on the corner of London Street, occupied in 1778 by the printer Robert Wetton, first became a chemist's shop in 1823 when John Boyce moved in. Agnew Nicholson took it over in 1901 and retired in 1950. It remained a chemist's until it was largely rebuilt in 1986. The large building, nos. 1-3 London Street, in the left foreground was once the premises of Joseph Sparrow, cabinet maker and auctioneer, who died in 1823. James Waterer of Woking, auctioneer, took over the building c. 1826 and rebuilt it in 1865, as seen here. Claud Waterer, estate agent, remained at no. 3 until 1985/6, but no. 1 later became Court's furniture showrooms. In front of these buildings can be seen the iron posts with rings formerly used for securing cattle on market days, this area being the original market place.

London Street From Windsor Street c. 1955

Although in many ways unaltered in the 35 years since T.L. Gadd had taken the photo above, this view shows the huge increase in private motoring. The Chertsey War Memorial had been dedicated in 1921, but perhaps the most striking change in the street scene is the loss of the top storey of nos. 1 and 3 London Street, caused by a fire in the late 1940s. No. 5 London Street, built as a carriage showroom for Charles Head in 1890 and later occupied by Waterer's from 1916 to c. 1936-7, was now for sale again after the departure of furniture removers P. A. Smith.

2 London Street, 1914

Members of one of the Volunteer Battalions of the East Surrey Regiment are pictured here as they halted en route from Walton-on-Thames, their haversack rations augmented by a barrel of ginger beer. The building to the left of the soldiers was a warehouse belonging to Agnew Nicholson, the chemist: it had previously housed the town's first electricity generator, and prior to that, a mineral water factory. It was demolished in 1986.

Long Humphries' Iron Works c. 1939

Chertsey's old police station in Gogmore Lane was acquired by William Herring in the 1860s for use as a foundry. Long Humphries & Co. bought the business in 1929 from the executors of his son, William Anthony Herring, who had died in 1901. They continued there until 1968, when it was leased to Harven Form, and subsequently became the Gane Foundry in 1970. The final casting took place in 1982, when Gane moved to Harefield, Middlesex; and the site was redeveloped in the mid-1980s. The turning and fitting shop with belt-driven machinery shown here was one of a number of departments at the works which continued the long tradition of metal-working craftsmanship in the town. Examples of Long Humphries' work, in particular municipal ironwork, may still be seen in many parts of the area.

J. J. Elliott's Shop c. 1925

James John Elliott took over the corn chandler's business on the corner of Gogmore Lane at 117 Guildford Street from James Taylor in the late 1890s. His widow and son Charles ran it for some time after his death, and it was then sold to T. Benham & Sons c. 1930. The shop remained a corn merchant's until C.D. Osborne & Sons left in December 1974. At the time of this photograph, the shop also sold bread made on the premises by James Cosson (left). It is seen here with the window decorated for Christmas by Ron Percey, who created the design at the front out of corn and seeds.

Chertsey Show c. 1920

Mr. P. J. "Joe" Hurley, driving J. J. Elliott's waggon in the trade turnout class at the Chertsey Show c. 1920, where it was "Highly Commended". The horse became enamoured of a mare on the other side of the arena, and his consequent behaviour prevented a higher placing! Mr. Hurley later started a taxi business from 71 Station Road in 1926 with a green Model T Ford. At the time, the only competition in Chertsey was two horse-drawn cabs. The business survived wartime requisitioning and shortages, and he was proud to boast that his cabs were the only ones out during a raid or blackout. He finally retired from taxi driving in 1980 after 54 years of plying for hire.

Guildford Street Looking South, 22nd June 1911

As in other towns, a patriotic display of flags greeted the Coronation of George V at a period when traffic conditions allowed the photographer to set up his tripod in the middle of the main street to record the scene! The Crown Brewery, on the far right, was still in the hands of Friary, Holroyd & Healy's brewery, Guildford, but it is doubtful whether it continued brewing after 1890. There had probably been a brewery here since about 1820, and certainly by 1845. On the left, the nearer shops hide the arched entrance to White Hart Yard just beyond. The old archway demolished in 1970 was the last relic of an inn which traded from at least the 1660s until 1788, and it is now recalled by the arched entrance to the Sainsbury Centre.

A Local Band c. 1905

This fine example of the work of the Addlestone photographer
F. Gould was possibly taken in White Hart Yard. It shows the
Chertsey Town Band, formed c. 1893, grouped with members of
the Laleham Band, with whom they often gave joint
performances. Their instruments include trumpets,
euphoniums, horns, clarinets, trombones and a sousaphone.
Seated behind the bass drum are, on the right wearing a cap, the
Bandmaster A.J. Allen, and on the left, Harry W. Tunnell, the
Principal Cornet, a former official trumpeter for the High Sheriff
of Surrey. Mr. Tunnell for many years celebrated the New Year
by playing cornet solos outside his house at Eastworth Road.
The band continued with varying fortunes until the outbreak of
the Second World War. Its present successor is The Genet
Group Band (Chertsey), previously known as the Chertsey &
Addlestone Band.

Guildford Street Looking North c. 1927

The King's Head inn on the left, although a 16th century
building, seems to have been trading only since the end of the
17th century. Although still in business, it has now lost the
nearer part of the building with the archway, which was
demolished about 1965. The archway led to a yard where, in
1902, stabling for 18 horses was available. Opposite the inn can
be seen the 17th century former Queen's Head, in business as
such from at least 1814 to 1914, but by this time occupied by
William Meek, confectioner.

Guildford Street Looking North c. 1908

The ices available from Ernest Hook, confectioner, in 1908 were undoubtedly made locally, perhaps by one of the Italian families resident in the Goosepool area. Beyond his shop on the left were the premises of Thomas Ashby, pork butcher; Emberson & Son, photographers; and Arthur Howard, pawnbroker, jeweller and silversmith. Opposite, to the right of The Queen's Head, which closed in 1914, was Bon Marche, a high-class draper's shop, run by Herbert Sawyer Harnett and his wife Ada Maria. The two ladies with the pram are standing outside the shop which had been occupied for some years by George Charles Slark, greengrocer, but at about this time passed into the hands of James Nelson & Sons, butchers.

Guildford Street Looking North, 1934/5

The newly-built shop of F.W. Woolworth in the right foreground replaced the old Queen's Head Inn. Beyond are the International Tea Co's. Stores, transferred from 129 Guildford Street between 1899 and 1905. The sign advertising the Tea Rooms belongs to Ruth's Pantry, run by Miss Ruth Edmonds, who married Mr. Longleather at about this time and continued trading until the early 1970s.

Harrowsmith's Shop c. 1905

Henry Blaker, father-in-law of Mrs. Blaker (see front cover), succeeded William Russell as town crier in the late 1890s. His son, Albert Henry, took over after his death in 1908. He is seen here outside Albert Harrowsmith's furniture shop at 77/79 Guildford Street. Mr. Harrowsmith's father had started the business in the mid-19th century. It closed c. 1910. Harrowsmith followed the old tradition of displaying goods on the pavement – what were then merely second-hand goods but would now be highly regarded as antiques! The premises beyond were rebuilt by George Wheeler, bookseller & newsagent, in 1885.

Guildford Street Looking North c. 1932

The Chertsey Cafe at 75 Guildford Street was run by Charles Brookson from the mid-1920s and remained in his family until at least 1945. Bernard D. Pearce, proprietor in the early 1940s, advertised that the cafe was recommended by the National Cycle Union (N.C.U.). Later it became "The Cat's Whisker" restaurant, run by J.E. Till. Harry Filmer Cook, corn merchant, operated from about 1930 from the premises once occupied by Albert Harrowsmith. Previously he had traded from Station Road and Windsor Street. Bates Brothers started business as hosiers and hatters shortly before the First World War at 78 Guildford Street. They remained in business until about 1970. The shop was demolished after a fire in 1974. No. 80, now the offices of Paine & Brettell, was originally the south pavilion of Burwood House, built in 1722 by a local doctor, Duncan Dundas.

Murray's Bookshop, 1947

Leslie and Constance Murray's shop at 3 Burwood Parade, opened c. 1944, had started life as a chemist's shop, Ascott's, built on part of the site of Burwood House c. 1936. As well as books, the shop sold toys and games, stationery and had a lending library. Mr. & Mrs. Murray were involved with the film industry before the Second World War; he as a camera technician, she as a dancer and make-up artist. Iris Hurley and Lily Kirby are seen examining part of the extensive stock carried at the time. Many of the new titles on show would now be highly regarded by book collectors.

Guildford Street Looking North c. 1910

In the foreground is Cowley House, formerly known as The Porch House, where the Royalist poet Abraham Cowley lived from 1665 until his death in 1667. The porch after which it had been named projected 10 ft. into the highway and was demolished in 1786 by the owner, Richard Clark, who commemorated it by erecting the plaque, seen on the front wall and now in Chertsey Museum. The house was rebuilt in 1870, but the original street front survived until 1927. The grounds of Beomonds, one of several large houses in Guildford Street, lay behind the wall on the right, on the site of the modern library and car park.

Guildford Street Looking North c. 1930

Following the demolition in 1927 of that part of the original Cowley House which still survived, a row of shops was erected on the site with gables reminiscent of that on the old building. On the left is the single-storey office of coal merchants Lowther & Little, who had moved from 111 Guildford Street. Albert Rope's cycle agency had formerly been at 88 Guildford Street. Next door at 59C were Brown & White, opticians, and no. 61 was occupied by greengrocer Robert Pyle. Various changes of use followed and these retail premises were lost to Chertsey when they were demolished in January 1978. Hanging over the street from the grounds of Beomonds, opposite, is a magnificent specimen of a false acacia tree which was for many years a feature of the street scene here.

Cowley House, 1935

Named after the Royalist poet who died in a house fronting Guildford Street in 1667, this imposing brick and stone house was built in 1870 for Charles Worthington in the fashionable ecclesiastical style of the time. This was greatly influenced by the widespread archaeological and church building activity throughout the land. Local work at the Abbey site had also added to the interest in mediaeval architecture, although the elaborate carved stonework and decorative brickwork had since been obscured by ivy. Later the home of John Augustus Tulk's family, Cowley House was split into five flats following Mrs. Tulk's death and also housed the accounts department of the Chase Cloche Company. The house was demolished in 1977 and the site is now occupied by a new development built in 1986.

Chertsey Brewery c. 1890

The Chertsey Brewery, which stood opposite the site now occupied by the public library, was in operation under John Keene from 1843, and possibly earlier, when his predecessors, the Wood family, ran a maltings here. It remained a working brewery until the latter half of the 1890s, the last brewers on the site being Richard Porter & Sons. The workers seen here are bottling pale ale, as indicated by the letters FPA on the casks. This was available at 1/2d (approximately 6p) per gallon in 1895-6. The bottles were of course returnable, and would be washed and re-used. The only surviving portion of the brewery premises is the empty building now named Caxton House at 57 Guildford Street. This was occupied from about 1908 to 1945 by Stevens & Son, printers.

Chertsey Hospital Flag Day, 1927

Posed outside the Congregational Church are volunteer flag sellers who were raising money for a cottage hospital. At this time, cases were referred either to Windsor or to the new hospital at Weybridge, and a Chertsey Hospital Fund with H. Farr as Treasurer and W.C. Billing as Hon. Sec. had been set up to build and maintain a cottage hospital in Chertsey. Although £123 6s 11d was raised by this and other efforts, it was felt that there was a lack of support for the venture in the town. In the event, the funds were used to provide an ambulance for the area, which came into use in April 1929. The Congregational Church had been built in 1876 by the Chertsey builders, T. & W. Knight. Opened for worship on 10th April 1877, the building has been used since September 1986 as a parish centre for St. Ann's Roman Catholic parish.

C.J. Nesmyth's Shop c. 1890

Charles Nesmyth was trading as a corn merchant from 36 Guildford Street by 1886, when the shop became home to the local sub-post office. In the late 1890s his business moved to 111 Guildford Street and the sub-post office transferred to Edward Stott's draper's shop next door at no. 34.

Southern Chertsey Looking South West, 1928

This aerial photograph by Aerofilms gives a good view of the area surrounding Chertsey Station. The goods yard can be seen in the left foreground with its goods shed and cattle pens in the corner of the photograph. The signal box, closed in 1974, stands beside the level crossing. This end of Station Road, open farmland in 1870, was laid out in the following decade, although the eastern end from a little west of Victory Road is of earlier date. T. Knight & Sons' works, with their large yard, are visible between Station Road and the goods yard. Other industrial premises include F.J. Thomas' coachbuilding works at 15-19 Guildford Street; the adjacent Thompson's smithy at no. 21; and the fire-damaged maltings in Fox Lane North, demolished in the 1960s. Beyond this can be seen the partly-built Barker Road development. At the upper left is Sir William Perkins' School, transferred to this site from Windsor Street in 1819. The present main school block, built in 1914, can be seen here.

Guildford Street Looking North c. 1908

With the exception of the demolition of Cowley House and the building of the Palace Cinema c. 1910, this view of Guildford Street taken in 1908 is little changed. The limited gas street lighting, augmented by shopkeepers' own illumination, was a necessity in the days when late night shopping was normal for the working population. George Bryan's single-storey oil and colour shop at no. 41 on the left was the equivalent of today's hardware store, selling household goods and paint, and had been established by 1886. He also ran a pawnbroker's shop at no. 43 and a lodging house behind the oil and colour shop.

Guildford Street Looking North c. 1914

In the right foreground can be seen Richard Maddox's stationer's shop with the owner and family in the doorway. As well as selling picture postcards, the shop acted as Chertsey's agency for Goss commemorative china. Next door at no. 30 were the premises of Alfred Stone & Sons, pork butchers and farmers at Stepgates Farm. The white gabled building in the left middle distance was the Electric Palace cinema, managed at this time by George Hall. It was in competition with the Constitutional Hall, then also used as a cinema, and in November 1913 was advertising the superior attractions of its tip-up seats and all-year-round opening.

Richard Moir's Staffordshire House c. 1910

37 and 39 Guildford Street, a late Georgian building called the "Victoria Stores", were run by members of the Moir family as a family baker and grocer. The Staffordshire House shown here was converted from the baker's at no. 39 by c. 1880. On sale were a wide variety of the products of the Stoke-on-Trent area, which brought cheap and attractive pottery to the mass market. As well as selling the jug and basin sets and jardinières, etc. pictured here, Moir's advertised "China and glass riveted on the premises by experienced workmen". Before the advent of suitable glues, this was the only practical method of repairing broken articles.

Guildford Street Looking South c. 1934

A butcher, a baker and a candlestick seller appear as neighbours in Guildford Street at the time this photograph was taken. At no. 30, William Leonard Weaver had taken over from Alfred Stone as a butcher. Pitcher & Co. were bakers at no. 32 and Mrs. Martha Maddox, bookseller and stationer at no. 28, continued as Chertsey's agent for Goss china, selling replicas of antiquities including candlesticks decorated with local crests. Street lighting had improved somewhat in 30 years and the local authority had erected two electric lights along this stretch of Guildford Street.

Edward Rowles and Sons c. 1909

In the days of coal and wood fires, regular visits from a sweep were essential. The Rowles family originated in the Staines area, and William Rowles was working as a sweep in Egham by the mid-1820s. Isaac, father of Edward Rowles, was listed as a chimney sweep at Goose Pool by 1861. Isaac's brother and nephew, both named Richard, operated as sweeps at Addlestone Moor, where they also ran "The Royal Oak" public house for some years. Edward is seen here with his sons Nelson (left) and George Ambrose outside their home at 1 Fox Lane North, which itself had a large inglenook fireplace. He died in 1943 aged 86, and was sweeping chimneys until the morning of the day he died. The house passed to Nelson, but George carried on the business there as his tenant until his death in 1957, when Nelson sold it to Fogarty's Motors. It was demolished soon afterwards.

The Fire Station, Goosepool, c. 1916

By the outbreak of the First World War, Chertsey's voluntary fire brigade had been established for over 100 years, as by 1811 the town already kept two horse-drawn fire engines in an engine house at the Queen's Head inn, at 2 guineas rent. In 1890 – the year of the construction of Addlestone Fire Station – a new fire station at Goosepool was built to replace earlier premises in London Street. Here, the brigade's Captain, J. J. Perrow, centre, can be seen engaged in rescue training for the local Scouts during the Great War. A report of 11th June 1909 had stated that many boys were joining the 1st Chertsey Scouts, bringing the total to "surpass a score", but the Scouter in charge was not given a warrant until 17th September 1909. The Group was finally registered in 1919, when Mr. Outer was Scout Master. It disbanded during the Second World War and was reformed in 1946 by Mr. A. J. Nichol.

Goosepool 1928

Chertsey, in common with many other low-lying areas of the Thames Valley, was subject to periodic floods. That of 1928 was less severe here than others, although many other Thames-side areas were badly affected. A combination of heavy snowfalls and a fast thaw led to this scene outside the fire station on 2nd January. Members of the brigade could at least demonstrate their equipment to the photographer and bystanders. Chertsey's fire engine, the "Curfew King", purchased from Dennis in 1926 for £1,165, can be seen on the right. The tender on the left is the converted Daimler lorry formerly owned by the Addlestone brigade and acquired c. 1920. In response to the localised flooding at Bell Corner and Goosepool, Chertsey Urban District Council agreed to spend £100 on building a new culvert. To the left of the fire station can be seen the Council Mortuary.

F.J. Thomas' Coach & Wheel Works c. 1910

Craftsmen and apprentices pose for the photographer outside the works of Frederick James Thomas at 15-19 Guildford Street. He had set up his business here in 1893, catering particularly for showmen and travellers, and soon became so renowned for his sturdy chassis, or "underworks", that showmen ordering living vans from builders in southern England often stipulated "Chertsey" or "Thomas'" unders. The upper floor of the two-storey building seen on the left of the works in the aerial view on page 21 was used for building the bodies of the vans, which were then brought down on rails and fixed to the underworks constructed downstairs. Besides caravans and carts, Thomas' works produced roundabouts, swingboats, ring boards and hoop-las, for which he held a patent.

Level Crossing c. 1929

Although it would be inadvisable to play with a hoop in the area of the railway crossing today, the street scene is little changed apart from the introduction of automatic barriers in October 1972. The milk churn on the left is a reminder of the days when milk from small dairy farms was routinely sent by rail to the major towns. A vital import via the railway system was coal, previously brought to the town by barge via the Thames: the opening of the branch line in 1848 allowed more widespread trade. On the right can be seen the long-established coal offices of E.A. Kimber, and of Lowther & Little, who also had premises at 59A Guildford Street. Another part of the railway revolution was the building of the Station Hotel in 1869, managed at this time by E. H. Thompson.

Atkins' Motor Cycle Works c. 1926

No. 11 Guildford Road, now demolished, had been Walter Williams' cycle agency until 1914, when Atkins & Penfold took over the premises. Herbert Atkins' son Stanley ran the business from c. 1924 to 1935. Apart from being an agent for many famous but now defunct brands of motor and pedal cycles, Stanley also sold petrol, ran a taxi and coach hire service and acted as Engineer for the voluntary fire brigade.

Guildford Road Looking North c. 1910

The Edwardian couple photographed by the Teddington photographers Young & Co. are posed outside the Cowley Almshouses. The central pair of almshouses, built in 1788 by Richard Clark of Cowley House, replaced a pair opposite the Vine Inn built in 1672-3 with money bequeathed by Abraham and Thomas Cowley. The flanking pair were added by Clark's son, the Rev. John Crosby Clark, c. 1870. In 1983 the whole block was painstakingly rebuilt by the Wickens Building Group.

Station Road c. 1910

Although primarily residential, Station Road by this time contained a wide range of trade premises and retail outlets. The Eastleigh Works of Thomas and James Knight, builders, on the right had moved from London Street and Bridge Road by 1902. Head's coach works had arrived by 1881. Station Road also housed a plumber, florist, costumier, second-hand clothes dealer, grocer, pub and chapel, and the area had a reputation for hard-working neighbourliness. Thomas Knight also acted from here as agent for the West Surrey General Benefit Society, one of the many organisations set up to help the working man and his family in time of need.

Harvest Festival c. 1912

Children and young people of the Primitive Methodist Church pose inside their chapel in Station Road. The festival was celebrated in great style, with the whole interior elaborately decorated for the thanksgiving services. The Primitive Methodists broke away from the main body of Methodism in 1811 and established separate circuits and organisation. Chertsey's congregation grew out of meetings at the home of Mr. James Brown. Mr. Johnson of Addlestone Moor gave the site for a chapel, which was opened on the first Sunday in April 1878. In 1936 the Wesleyan and Primitive Methodists came together to form the present church, and Chertsey's congregation then worshipped at the London Street site church. The building in Station Road is now used by the Jehovah's Witnesses.

Street Party, Station Road, 1945

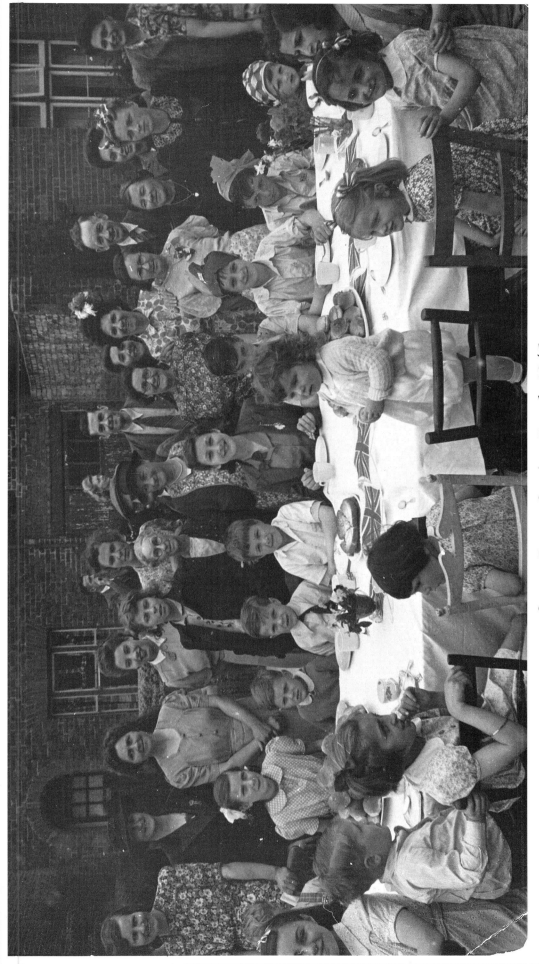

The official end of the war in Europe, "V.E. Day" 8th May 1945, was marked with spontaneous celebrations across the country. Amongst these were the fondly-remembered street parties, and the Chertsey area was the scene of many of these events. That held in Station Road was typical of the arrangements. After nearly six years of war and the absence of many husbands and fathers on active service, peace was celebrated in style: in spite of the scarcity of many items, an impressive array of food was prepared; although one resident recalls the substitution of liquid paraffin for strictly-rationed fats in pastry and cakes! Station Road also celebrated with dancing in the street and a sing-song around a piano brought out into the street. Those shown include: (standing): Mrs. Pollard, Miss Fraser, Mrs. Inskip, Doreen Roake, Beryl Kent, ?, ?, Jimmy Smithers, ?, Mr. Witts, Mrs. Edwards, Mrs. Witts?, Lucy Pucci, ?, Mr. Lewis, ?, ?, ?, Mrs. Strutt: (seated): Yvonne, Robert & Roy Inskip, Johnny Hollick, June Roake, Brian and Terry Inskip, 2 evacuees?, Jimmy & Jean Heather, Marion Patterson, ? Strutt?, ?, Marion & Joan Ballerino.

29

Eastworth Road Looking East, 1911

A traffic-free road enabled residents to pose for one of Gorrad's many fine photographs of the area taken to commemorate the Coronation of George V. The premises in the left foreground at no. 9 were occupied at this time by Hunt & Sons, builders, later Boast's sanitary engineers and undertakers.

Funeral of Mr. Perrow, 28th June 1929

John James Perrow was born in Cornwall, but came to Chertsey with his family in 1871. He was a lifelong member of the Wesleyan Methodist Church, holding many offices in the church and local organisations. When young, he worked for Claude Waterer, and later as a pattern maker at Herring's Iron Foundry, where his father worked in the attached shop. He joined the local fire brigade in 1889, becoming Chief Officer in 1905, and in all attended 361 fires. His son Frederick George followed in his footsteps, becoming a call-boy in the days of the horse-drawn steam fire engine and remaining in the Chertsey Brigade until March 1932. The traditional fireman's funeral transport, a decorated engine, was used: in this case Chertsey's "Curfew King", followed by the Addlestone appliance, and over 70 firemen from 16 brigades attended Chertsey's popular and highly-regarded Fire Chief.

School of Handicrafts Farm c. 1910

The School of Handicrafts was established in Eastworth Road by Thomas Hawksley M.D. at a cost of £25,000, following a public meeting at the Society of Arts on 11th November 1885 "for the purpose of inaugurating an industrial school on self-supporting principles, with the double object of turning out thoroughly efficient workmen and of maintaining the school as far as possible by the productive value of the industries taught, carried out on a business scale." The first pupils arrived in March 1887. The boys, who remained at the school from the age of eight until they were apprenticed at thirteen, were taught a wide variety of trades including agriculture, gardening, carpentry, smithying, bricklaying, painting, cabinet-making, plumbing and printing. They built their own workshop and made their own boots. The boys also had a band, which was a familiar sight on its weekly march to St. Peter's Church.

School of Handicrafts, January 1915

This view of some of the pupils at the School of Handicrafts in the fields attached to the school clearly demonstrates the reason for the long delay in developing the northern side of Eastworth Road. While there is now housing at the eastern end, this area is still playing fields and remains liable to flooding. The flood recorded here reflects the severe effects of the bad weather at the beginning of January 1915, when gales and heavy rain caused the Thames to rise rapidly to its third highest recorded level, flooding many areas of low-lying ground.

Lyne, Longcross and Ottershaw

This map is reproduced from the 6 in. Ordnance Survey map as revised in 1912 and published in 1920.

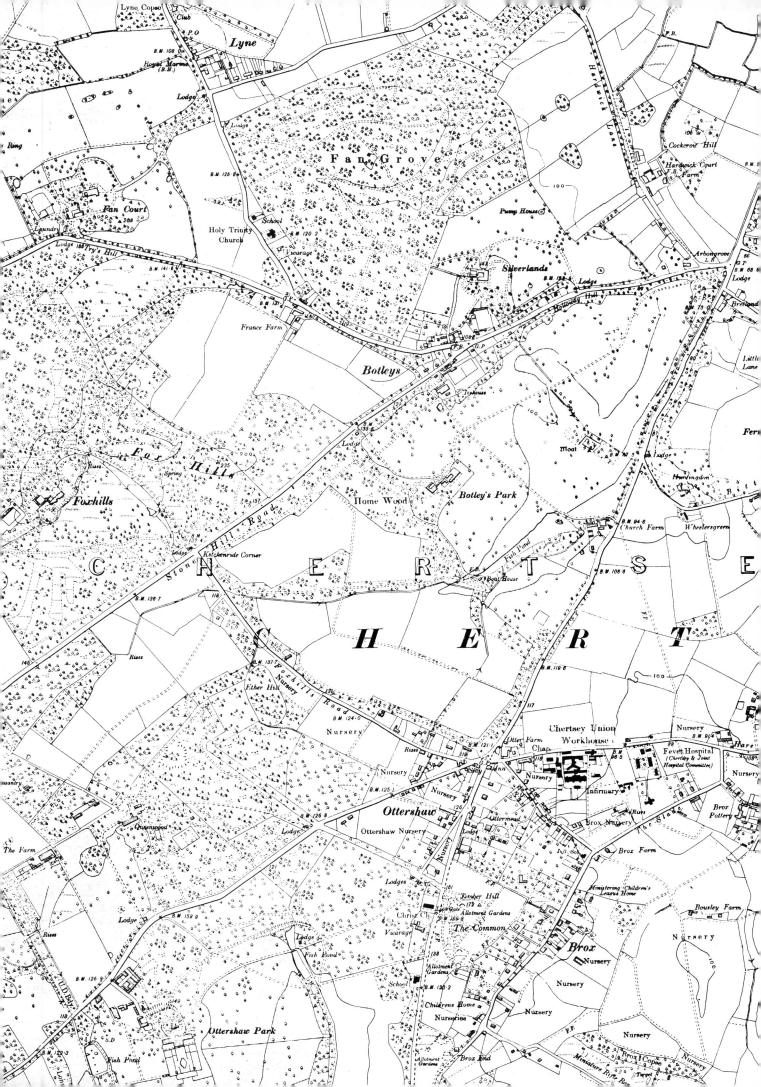

All Saints' Church c. 1910

Now occupied by a block of flats, the site on the corner of Victory Road was formerly home to the fine red brick Anglican church dedicated to All Saints. Its foundation stone had been laid on 27th September 1900, and it was built on part of the garden of Chertsey grocer Richard Moir at No. 1 Laburnum Villas. Falling congregations and rising expenses led to its closure: the last service was held in November 1971 and the church demolished in 1975.

All Saints' Church Interior c. 1910

The fine quality of the craftsmanship can be gauged from this view of the interior. It was built at a cost of nearly £7,000, with major subscriptions coming from local dignitaries, including William Herring, Frederick Lowten Spinks and Manwaring Shurlock. The church was originally lit by gas, and a visitor in 1910 recorded the rail-back benches of deal, wood block floor and oak pulpit, and provision for a south aisle to be added later.

Highfield School, Chertsey.   28.

Highfield School c. 1910

Although now Salesian Community House, this school originally
operated from the 1880s as the "Highfield House Middle Class
Boarding School" with William Tranter, a relative of the Vicar of
Egham, as Principal. A popular subject for picture postcards of
the time, the school suffered varying fortunes during the First
World War. In 1914 there were 28 boys in residence, and by
1917 the site had been sold to Kent Coast College, Herne Bay,
after they had been bombed out. The school was eventually
rented by the Salesian Order in August 1922.

St. Ann's Chapel, Eastworth House, c.1910

A Roman Catholic chapel was originally erected on the St. Ann's
Hill estate of Charles James Fox's great nephew, the 4th Baron
Holland. Its chaplain was the retired rector of St. Charles
Borromeo, Weybridge, Father Charles Comberbach. This chapel,
in the grounds of Eastworth House, was built c.1899 by the
Salesian Sisters who had just moved there. It continued in use
until a larger building at Highfield School was adapted for use.
The present St. Ann's Catholic Church opened for worship in
July 1930.

St. Ann's Catholic Church, Chertsey.   Southern Series. 27-B.

Chertsey Police Station, 1911

Compared with many other buildings in the area, the County Police Station was rather sparsely decorated for the Coronation of George V. The building was also the home of Superintendent Thomas Mears and his family. Chertsey's original police station had been in Gogmore Lane and was later incorporated into the Herring's foundry building. The building shown here was erected in the mid-1860s.

Chertsey Urban District Council Refuse Vehicle, 1936

The Chertsey Urban District Council grew out of various bodies charged with organising local services such as lighting, sanitation and highways. Originally based on committees run by parish officers, the local government reorganisation of 1894 brought together these various functions under the control of a network of urban and rural district councils. The Chertsey Urban District Council remained until its amalgamation with the Egham Urban District Council, forming the Runnymede District Council, in 1974. Part of the responsibility of the original Rural Sanitary Authority was the collection of refuse, or "scavenging", and to facilitate this, a new horse-drawn dust cart had been purchased in 1885 for £25.10s. The Council depot in Fordwater Road was purchased by Chertsey Urban District Council in 1934, and complemented that in Pyrcroft Road, originally established in 1902. In 1936 the new vehicle shown here was bought from the specialist builder Dennis of Guildford. With a capacity of 10 cubic yards, the latest word in motorised refuse collection cost the ratepayers £525.

Fordwater Road c. 1930

This part of Fordwater Road was included in the area originally known as Stepgates – hence the sign "Stepgates Post Office" on the sub-post office and general store, then run by Walter Aldworth and still in business today. The post office had opened in 1911 in the northern half of a pair of semi-detached houses called Derby Villas, built in 1865. A former resident, born in Fordwater Road in 1903, recalled the shop where, before the First World War, it was possible to buy anything from paraffin to a pennyworth of cheese. Edmund Denyer, whose van can be seen parked beyond the car on the left, had a grocer's shop at 40 Guildford Street. Most of the houses seen on the right date to the 1890s.

Stepgates From Mead Lane c. 1919

The name "Stepgates" originally referred to the surrounding area rather than to a street, but by 1920 this was marked on the map as Stepgates Road. The two corner shops were built in the early 1890s before the development of the rest of what was then a country lane, and at the time of this early photograph by Thomas Gadd they retained their original character as a baker's and a general store, despite both having changed hands. John A. Guthrie, baker and confectioner, remained here from about 1914 until his death in the early 1940s, but Charles Brown's shop had passed into the hands of Bertram Edward Light by 1919. The flags decorating Mr. Guthrie's premises suggest that the photograph was taken during the peace celebrations of that year.

Empire Day, Stepgates Girls' School, 1912

The celebration of "Empire Day" was conceived by a local resident, the Earl of Meath, who lived at Ottermead, Ottershaw. First held on 24th May 1903, the anniversary of Queen Victoria's birth, it became an established event in school calendars. Elaborate pageants and displays extolling the virtues of the then British Empire were held regularly until the 1950s, when the event became Commonwealth Day. Here some of the 300 girls at the school, listen attentively to patriotic speeches under the watchful eyes of the school mistress, Miss Jane McCaig, and local dignitaries.

Stepgates Football Team 1914

Boys and staff pose with the school's newly-won trophy, the "Sparrow Shield". The Headmaster, John Francis Baily (left), had previously been in charge of Sir William Perkins' School. Stepgates Council School, built in 1908 to cater for the area's rapidly-growing population, had places for 400 boys and 400 girls, as well as an infants' department. Stepgates boys were regularly successful in this competition organised in the N.W. Surrey area, and its junior players went on to become members of many local football clubs, including Chertsey Town, founded in 1890.

Pound Pond c. 1910

The Pound Pond, originally created as a result of early gravel workings, stretched along the eastern side of Pound Road from the spot shown, just south of the London Street corner, almost to the corner of Stepgates, where the Horsell Farm buildings stood until the early 1960s. The local pound for stray animals, after which it was named, lay opposite the farm on the other side of the road. It is reported that visiting circuses, as well as local farmers, used the pond to water their animals. Carts would also be driven through to swell the wooden wheels in order to keep their tyres tight in hot weather.

Chertsey Volunteers c. 1875

Following a request from the Secretary of State for War, Lord Palmerston, in 1859 in the face of a possible threat from France, Volunteer forces were established in many parts of the country. A standing committee of local worthies with Henry Grazebrook as Hon. Sec. was convened, and Chertsey formed the 15th Surrey Rifle Volunteer Corps. Members paid an annual subscription of 1 guinea and bought their own distinctive uniform and accoutrements, as seen here. After December 1897, they were designated the 3rd Volunteer Battalion the East Surrey Regiment, and as such saw action in the Boer War.

Chertsey Home Guard, 1941

In answer to a more recent threat from Hitler's Wehrmacht to Britain's sovereignty, Chertsey men again answered the call to defend the country and their home area. Members of Chertsey Company 6th Battalion East Surrey Home Guard pose outside the Drill Hall built in 1902. Home Guard troops were drawn from those over or under the age for regular service and those engaged on war work. Although affectionately portrayed as "Dad's Army", the lightly-armed volunteers were highly motivated and ready to fight if an invasion came. Ray Lowther, subsequently a long-serving Chertsey councillor, (fourth from left in the front row), recalls: "Everyone was extremely enthusiastic. We mounted guard at the Drill Hall, St. Peter's Church tower, the telephone exchange in Guildford Street, the waterworks, and at Woburn Hill, not far from the anti-aircraft battery on what is now the Meadowlands Mobile Home Park. In addition, there was a bicycle patrol through Chertsey, Thorpe and Lyne."

St. Peter's Church, 29th March 1919

A church or chapel has existed on this site, near the gates of Chertsey Abbey, since at least 1198. Originally dedicated to All Saints, it became St. Peter's after the Abbey was dissolved in 1537. The present building dates mainly to 1806-8, although the old tower and chancel were retained with alterations. The original architect was Richard Elsam, but the building was completed by Thomas Chawner following some malpractice on Elsam's part. The total cost was about £12,000. The town pump in front of the church was given by John Ivatt Briscoe of Foxhills in 1863. It was moved back from its original position in the roadway c. 1970.

Bellringing at St. Peter's Church, 1947

A scene from the Central Office of Information film: "Come Saturday", made for the Foreign Office to show how British people entertained themselves on Saturdays. Chertsey's peal of eight bells includes several of historical interest: the fifth, or "Abbey", bell was cast in 1310 for Chertsey Abbey, and recast in 1380 after being damaged when the bell-tower collapsed. At the Dissolution, it was transferred to the parish church. The tenor and sixth bell were made in Chertsey; the sixth in 1712 by William Eldridge, and the tenor in 1670 by Bryan Eldridge. The tenor was recast in 1859. Chertsey still observes the ancient custom of ringing the curfew, or "couvre-feu", (literally "cover fire"), originally instituted as a safety measure.

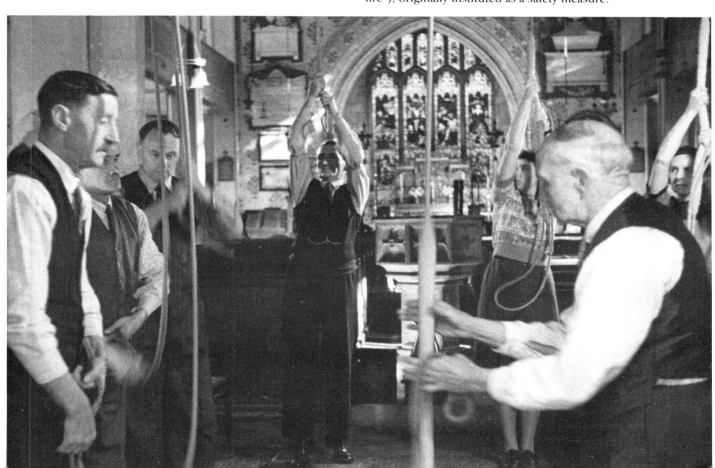

Chertsey Looking South c. 1910

Looking south from the tower of St. Peter's Church can be seen Guildford Street's interesting assortment of roofs and chimneys. No doubt many of the tiles and bricks used were the products of the local industry which utilised the area's clay beds. In contrast, the fields behind stretch as far as Eastworth Road, the southern side of which was almost completely developed by 1910. The spire of All Saints' Church can be seen below the horizon a little to the right of centre.

Madeley's Grocery Shop, 26th February 1921

No. 5 Windsor Street had been a grocer's shop from 1854, Edward Taylor Madeley taking over in the late 1860s. By 1899 the firm also had premises in Addlestone, Egham, Weybridge, Walton-on-Thames and Queen's Road, Peckham. Typical of establishments of the time, Madeley's offered personal service, home delivery and expert departments for the wide range of goods offered. The characteristic window display also illustrates the availability of convenience foods even at that date: in this case, pancake mix! By 1961 the business had been taken over by T. Edwards, and was rebuilt and modernised.

Women's War Work, April 1918

The Women's War Work Committee instigated by Mrs. and Miss Savory of Sandgates, Guildford Road, was organised to produce comforts for members of the armed forces. Socks and balaclavas were knitted and collections made of money, eggs, fruit and vegetables for men in local war hospitals. The ladies also met troop trains which stopped at Chertsey Station and dispensed tea and buns to the soldiers. From November 1915 they met at 21 Windsor Street, previously Percy Longley's, a cabinet maker. Here they produced many thousands of articles for distribution to local men in the armed forces. Immediately after the war the premises were used by Thomas Gadd and his wife, photographers who toured the district on bikes and produced many fine views of the area from their "Gresham Studios". Mrs Gadd ran a kindergarten there in the 1950s.

Chertsey Jubilee Procession, 1935

As part of the celebration of the 25-year reign of King George V and Queen Mary, a procession was organised in the town. St. Peter's bells were pealed for an hour on the morning of 6th May and the parade lined up at Free Prae Road in the afternoon. Hundreds of adults and children in fancy dress accompanied the Jubilee Queen, Rita Smith, and her attendants, together with the Fire Brigade, Chertsey Ambulance and numerous decorated trade vehicles. Later, at a tea for 1,111, gifts of propelling pencils and chocolate were presented to the town's children – a gift from Lord Camrose. The celebrations continued during the day, and in the evening the Town Band led the way to St. Ann's Hill, where further festivities, including maypole dancing, were held. A bonfire lit at 10.00 p.m. on the summit was one of a national chain of such beacons uniting the country in its celebration. The procession led by the Town Band is seen passing William Worley's Abbey Dairy. Beyond, at no. 20, is Harold Proctor's fish and chip shop. The white house on the far right is the Snow White Laundry, demolished in 1974.

Chertsey Jubilee Procession. 1.
May 6th 1935.

Rawlings & Walsh c. 1927

Workers from Rawlings & Walsh gather outside their offices for a charabanc trip to the south coast. Thomas J. Rawlings, master printer, was living with his parents in the house on the corner of Alwyns Lane in 1871. From here he published the "Surrey Advertiser & County Times" from c. 1882, and the first "Surrey Herald" on 4th June 1892. Rawlings & Walsh Ltd. was formed in 1900, Marshall Walsh being the first Editor of the Surrey Herald. The printing was carried out in the premises in Alwyns Lane behind the house, but later the former Weston House coachhouse on the corner of Colonel's Lane was used as their printing works until 1960. The pair of 18th century houses seen here were demolished and replaced by a new building in 1934.

Windsor Street Looking North West c. 1950

The Swan Inn in the left foreground dates from at least the late 16th century, when it was known as The White Swan, and was Chertsey's principal coaching inn in the 18th and 19th centuries. In Queen Victoria's reign, royal coaches would stop here to change horses en route between Windsor Castle and Claremont House in Esher. For this reason the landlord, former Police Superintendent William Henry Biddlecombe, was the first man in Chertsey to hear of the death of Prince Albert in December 1861, when the Duke of Nemours stopped there on his way to Windsor Castle. Beyond the early 18th century Denmark House can be seen the "Surrey Herald" offices, demolished in 1988 and replaced by the present Alwyn House.

Chertsey From the North West c. 1925

An aerial view of the northern part of Chertsey, looking across the Abbey Forefield in the foreground, along Windsor Street and London Street. Abbey House, demolished in 1964, is visible in the left foreground, and beyond it and the area now occupied by Abbey Gardens is the field known as The Hollows. On the far side of Colonel's Lane is the site of New House, home of Sir William Perkins: He bequeathed it to Henry Weston, after whom it was renamed Weston House. It was demolished c. 1825, but the coach house survives on the corner of Colonel's Lane and Windsor Street.

Grove Road, 1894

A serious flood affected Chertsey during November 1894 and much of the town was inundated. Following heavy rains, the rising waters of the Thames and local streams combined and from Friday 16th November many streets were flooded to a depth of 2 ft. or more. Much inconvenience and damage was suffered and, following the subsidence of the water by the 21st, a flood relief committee was set up to provide assistance to those affected. As well as financial help, over 230 sacks of coal were distributed to over 100 homes. The scene in Grove Road was recorded by W. Bates in one of many photographs taken at the time.

Hamperstone Bridge c. 1905

This small bridge in St. Ann's Road near Twynersh now lies in a cul-de-sac created by the construction of the dual carriageway to Staines, but at this time there was no major road here, the original Staines Lane having started at the end of Windsor Street.

The Golden Grove c. 1900

Standing in Ruxbury Road on the lower slopes of St. Ann's Hill, The Golden Grove probably dates from the 17th century. By the 19th century, St. Ann's Hill had a reputation as a local beauty spot, and the inn was a popular haunt of visitors requiring refreshment. Many people liked to have their drinks served in the large tree house in the lower branches of the old elm tree near the road. The tree house was removed about 1945, but the tree survived, although rotten and hollow, until 1973 when it fell victim to Dutch elm disease. The landlord at this time, James Pullen, had arrived in the late 1890s and left c. 1902. Charles Hill Foster has here captured the inn with an assortment of vehicles outside, including a horse-drawn bus, a forerunner of the charabanc popular with "beanfeasters" on trips from the Metropolis. Extra horses were kept here to assist in pulling vehicles up the steep hill.

The Grange Hospital, Chertsey
Vice President — Lady Hutton,
Commandant — Hon. Le Mrs Blyth,
Matron — Mrs Miller.

The Grange War Hospital, 1916

Formerly known as The Hollies, and at one time the residence of the composer Sir George Smart, The Grange was for many years the home of the Brettell family, who were prominent in many aspects of Chertsey's public life. In 1915 Vivian Brettell made the house available as a war hospital, where between 30th January 1915 and 27th January 1919 many hundred walking wounded and convalescent battlefield casualties were treated. Local people provided many fittings for this use and generously supported collections of eggs, fruit and cigarettes for the soldiers. The building now continues the caring tradition as a retirement home.

Chase Cloches, The Grange, c. 1950

Founded in 1912 by Lloyd Heber Chase, an Australian civil engineer, to sell his invention "the Chase Continuous Cloche", the company moved to Chertsey about 1922. Originally based at Pound Pond, the firm also used sites at Gogmore Farm and Lyne as trial grounds and nurseries. The site at The Grange was acquired c. 1941 and used until 1961. As well as establishing the commercial and amateur use of the cloche system, Chase's also pioneered non-toxic and organic horticultural techniques developed at Chertsey and now in use worldwide. The company is still based in the Borough of Runnymede as part of the Ian Allan Group.

The presentation of St Ann's Hill. Chertsey. 1928.

Opening Ceremony, St. Ann's Hill, 1928

Public access to the popular summit area of St. Ann's Hill seemed to be threatened by the auction of the Hon. Stephen Powys' estates in July 1925. 20 acres were purchased by the West Surrey Water Society in the area adjacent to the ground which they already owned. In an act of great public-spiritedness,

however, Sir William Berry of Barrow Hills, Longcross, later Lord Camrose, purchased 16½ acres from them and presented the area, together with a further 7½ acres, to the Chertsey Urban District Council for use as a public recreation ground. After clearance and landscaping, the site was officially handed over by Lady Berry on 13th June 1928. At the ceremony, attended by the Chertsey Town Band and the Town Crier, the assembled crowds also heard a speech by Neville Chamberlain, then Minister for Health.

Lyne Railway Bridge 1978

Construction of Lyne's railway bridge landmark started in June 1976, and it was opened to traffic on February 12th 1979. The contract, carried out by RDL Contracting Ltd., called for a structure to carry the heaviest main line trains over the new M25 motorway then under construction. The building of one of the world's first all-concrete cable-stayed railway bridges also involved the temporary diversion of the railway between Chertsey and Virginia Water. The bridge's twin concrete towers, 22 metres high and supporting two 55 metre skew spans give Lyne a distinctive addition to the local skyline.

The Study, Silverlands, 1910

One of two from an album of photographs taken in 1910 by William Bates for the then owner, Sir John Brunner, and now in Chertsey Museum; this interior shows his study, which faced south, offering a fine view across the park. The room was 18 ft. 9 in. square, and the "walnut" panelling shown here was in fact made of plaster! Note the early telephone on the desk, and the directories on the shelves, including Burke's Peerage and Crockford's Clerical Directory. The Rt. Hon. Sir John Tomlinson Brunner was Chairman of Brunner, Mond & Co., Ltd., Alkali Manufacturers. He had been Liberal M.P. for Northwich, Cheshire from 1885 to 1886 and 1887 to 1909, a Privy Councillor in 1906, and created Baronet in 1895. He acquired Silverlands from Philip Waterlow in 1907-8, and died in 1919.

Silverlands, 1910

J. G. Thurlow, chauffeur to Sir John Brunner of Silverlands in Lyne, was captured by William Bates as he waited outside the north front of the house in the Rolls Royce. The name "Silverlond" was in use in 1420 to describe this piece of land, but the original house is thought to have been built by local brewer Robert Porter after 1814, and it was probably altered or rebuilt in the 1820s by Vice Admiral Sir Henry Hotham, who established the estate. Its main entrance was from Holloway Hill. The house was used as a war hospital in the First World War, and for many years from 1938 was the home of The Actors' Orphanage, founded in Croydon in 1895 for "destitute children of actors and actresses". It had moved to Langley Hall in Bucks. in May 1915, but by 1938 the many activities necessitated more extensive accommodation. It is now a nurses' training school.

White Lodge c. 1906

These elegant neo-classical lodge gates to Botleys Park were built in the early 19th century. Later, the gatekeeper's cottage was added behind the left-hand portico. Popularly known as White Lodge, its gates were demolished c. 1950 after the grounds were taken over by the National Health Service. Their name is preserved by the highly-regarded centre for the handicapped which opened in 1962. On the left can be seen the house then named Bretlands, the home of Miss Blunt, whose family had lived there since the 1830s. The house was demolished c. 1960 and Sandalwood Avenue built on the site.

Botleys Park, 1940

At the time of the Munich Crisis in 1938, plans were drawn up to provide hospital accommodation for the expected mass casualties of a war. The London teaching hospitals were the basis of a scheme to divide the South East into sections. Botleys Park came within Section VIII and was taken over by St. Thomas's. "Botleys Park Colony for Mental Defectives" had been officially opened on 24th June 1939, but at the outbreak of war was requisitioned and became known as "Botleys Park War Hospital". The first wounded soldier of the war was received here, and by February 1940, 500 casualties from France had been admitted. Botleys Park was the scene of some of the earliest use of the first antibiotic, penicillin, and a unit under Professor Flory was established. Queen Elizabeth came to Botleys Park on 28th May 1940 and, accompanied by the Matron, Miss C. Morris, and the Medical Superintendent, Dr. K. Paddle, visited Dunkirk survivors being treated here.

St. Peter's Hospital, Botley's Park, c. 1947

What is now known as St. Peter's Hospital was originally built as an emergency war hospital in the grounds of the Botley's Park Colony. Building started in 1939 and by 1941 some of the wards were completed. Twenty of these were built around a central open corridor, and were 140 ft. long and 24 ft. wide. Its first Medical Superintendent, Major General J.A. Manifold, C.B. D.S.O., and other medical officers of the time gave their names to some of the wards. When completed, Botleys Park War Hospital, apart from sharing certain facilities, was completely independent of the mental institution, and started taking local civilian patients at the end of the war. In 1946 the hospital finally separated from Botleys, becoming St. Peter's, and was transferred to the new National Health Service on 5th July 1948.

The Anchor, Botleys, 1938

This house on the north side of Botleys Green, which lies at the junction of Holloway Hill, Stonehill Road and Longcross Road, was formerly a public house called The Anchor. It was certainly trading as a public house by March 1770, and the building is probably of early 18th century date. The Anchor ceased trading about 1890 and became a private house, still called Anchor House. The building was part of the Silverlands estate until its sale in 1938.

Lyne Church c. 1910

Holy Trinity, the parish church of Botleys and Lyne, was built at a cost of £4,585.5s.4d. in 1849. The site had been given by Lady Frances Hotham of Silverlands, and the architect F. Francis designed in Early English style a church with chancel, nave, transepts and central tower. The ecclesiastical commentator Philip Palmer of Guildford, writing in 1910, records a visit to the church in July of that year. After describing Lyne as "a land of large estates, parks and woodlands", he notes the "exquisitely-kept churchyard with little flower gardens in the well-cut turf" – although the interior, he complained, was "ostentatiously plain", with no altar cross or candles.

Longcross School c. 1910

The parish of Longcross was formed from part of the parish of Chertsey in 1847, when Christ Church was built and endowed by the principal local landowner, William Tringham. The parochial school was also built in 1847 by William Tringham on land purchased from Mr. Grazebrook, the Chertsey solicitor. It was enlarged in 1852 and again in 1905 with places for 120 children. It closed in 1933, the number on the register having fallen as low as 25. The children were transferred to Lyne School, and the building turned into cottages. Mr. George Copeland, Master for 38 years, who also acted as Organist at Longcross Church, was assisted at this time by Miss Jane Crowhurst.

Festival of Britain Celebrations, Longcross House, 1951

Longcross children enjoy a Punch and Judy show in the grounds of Longcross House: part of the entertainment put on in celebration of the Festival of Britain then taking place at London's South Bank. The house was built by Major Charles Micklem D.S.O. to replace a smaller house pulled down in 1931.

Bridge-Laying Trials, Longcross, 1943

Between the wars, Carden Lloyd's works at Bridge Wharf, Chertsey, were involved in the design and testing of an amphibious light tank and other vehicles. These were taken to be tested at nearby Chobham Common, which had the joint advantages of isolation and a wide range of terrain, including peat bogs, ponds and sand hills. At the outbreak of war in 1939, the establishment known colloquially as "the Tank Factory" was established and a new station built on the Staines & Wokingham line. Extensive design and research facilities were erected, and much specialised armour and bridging equipment used in the liberation of Europe was developed at Longcross. Photographed in September 1943 at the "Fighting Vehicle Proving Establishment", a group of British and Russian officers attend a demonstration of the "Covenanter" bridge layer and its "Scissors" bridge.

Heath Cottage, Longcross Road, 1982

This cottage on the edge of Chobham Common was, until c. 1874, a beerhouse, The Travellers' Friend, run by the Mepham family, who also farmed the land surrounding the cottage and 18 acres on the other side of the road (later Heathlands). It was eventually purchased and delicensed by William Tringham, who built Longcross Church and gave the parish its Vicarage. The building was later known as Heath Cottage. It was empty at the time of this photograph, and was subsequently demolished.

The Otter c. 1922

The Otter had opened in 1803, and its first licensee was Samuel Neville, who also worked as a carpenter. By 1846 it had become the headquarters of the local branch of "The Friendly Brothers Society", one of many similar bodies, often based at licensed premises, formed during the industrial revolution to provide mutual assistance before the days of the welfare state. Standing outside, in this view by T. L. Gadd, is George Hall (second from the left), who was Manager from c. 1920 to c. 1925. He had formerly spent many years as landlord of The Black Horse, Bermondsey, and finding The Otter somewhat quiet, he decided to boost trade by serving teas in the attractive garden beside the inn. He also became Captain of the Ottershaw Cricket Club.

The Otter c. 1928

Frederick L. Latham took over The Otter from George Hall c. 1925, and soon afterwards a petrol pump was installed in front of the building in response to the rise of private motoring. In 1927, in common with many other suitably sited public houses, the inn was demolished and rebuilt as seen here, further back from the crossroads. The single pump is visible beside the inn sign. Frederick Latham also seems to have supplemented his income by keeping pigs, as an advert in the "Surrey Herald" of 30th April 1930 reads: "Sows & store pigs wanted. Best prices given. Manure 15/- per ton in 2 ton loads. Pig manure 12/6d in 2 ton loads." His daughter Myrtle married Wallace Victor England (known as Victor), who succeeded him as licensee c. 1936, and remained until his death in 1970. The Otter was purchased by Trust House Forte in 1983 and converted into the present Harvester Restaurant.

Roake's Smithy, 1908

Situated at an increasingly busy crossroads, the forge run by Henry Roake and his son Henry was much photographed during the first decades of this century. Its position also encouraged its use as a billboard for local sales and events. Henry Roake Junior (left) died in 1942. His daughter had married Arthur Thomas, son of F. J. Thomas of Guildford Street, Chertsey, and he used the former smithy after his father-in-law's death for building holiday caravans, ceasing in 1950. In common with many other sites formerly associated with blacksmiths or farriers, the building now houses its modern counterpart – in this case Raymond Slade Autos.

Ottershaw Post Office c. 1910

The first postal service in the Ottershaw area seems to have been established in 1844 at the home of James Coulton in Guildford Road. From the early 1890s Mr. George Rose had taken over the site and was also a draper and grocer. The post office moved to Brox Road in 1912 and the building has now been replaced by 1-4 The Hollies. Ottershaw's recently-arrived telephone service is indicated by the pole on the right, although the smartly uniformed telegraph boy could deliver or collect messages for transmission via the widespread network of the time.

Ottershaw Post Office.

The Gardeners' Arms Garage c. 1935

Opened as a beerhouse in the mid-19th century, The Gardeners' Arms survived until the death of the landlord, Benjamin Hyde, in 1931. His widow may have carried on for a short time after his death, but the pub was delicensed and sold in December 1933. At this time the premises boasted three bedrooms, a tap room, public bar, bar parlour, living room, scullery and large beer cellar, gas and electric light and an "excellent well water supply", together with nearly two acres of ground with fruit trees, etc., and a storage shed. It was acquired by Mr. Pat Hetherman, who converted it into a garage, filling station and tearoom, as seen here. The site is now part of the Trident Garage.

Christ Church, Ottershaw, c. 1895

The original decorative polychrome brickwork of the church is clearly seen here in a view of the east end before the insertion of the rood screen in 1896 and the reredos added in 1901, which obscures the central window. The church relied on candelabra for lighting until 1920, when gas lights were installed, and a visitor in 1910 commented: "The interior is elaborate but too dark even to distinguish the numbers of the hymns."

Christ Church, Ottershaw, c. 1875

This view by George Ward, who was working from Weybridge from at least 1873 to 1892, shows the church before the addition of the lych gate in 1881 and the tower and belfry in 1885. The pony and trap in which Ward carried his photographic equipment can be seen in the road in front of the church. Christ Church was built by Sir Thomas Edward Colebrook of Ottershaw Park in 1864.

Christ Church Choir 1937

This photograph, taken on the occasion of Henry Roake's completion of 60 years' service in the choir, shows the ladies in the new robes introduced by the Rev. Hiam, who had come to Christ Church in 1935. The choir members are, from left to right: (men) Alan Bates, Cyril Wade, Henry Roake, Stanley Yeandle (Organist/Choirmaster), Mr. Clare, Rev. Dudley Hiam, Bill Underwood (Verger), Bill Ottaway, Ralph Reeve; (women) Winnie Lawrence, Margaret Croxford, Mrs. Collier, Elsie Underwood, Mrs. Pharo, Mollie Bates, Jane Underwood, Louisa Thompson; (boys) ? Frusher, Raymond Ottaway, Ernie Pelling and George Hale.

Ottershaw Vicarage c. 1914

Christ Church's original vicarage was also built at the expense of Sir Edward Colebrooke, and at the time of this picture the living had a yearly value of £290 for the incumbent, the Rev. Percy Roberts Phillips. The vicarage had ten bedrooms, stabling and a coach house. The distinctive style of diaper-patterned brickwork was also used at Chertsey Vicarage, built in 1858. Proving too large for the parish at the time, the building was sold in 1934 and a new vicarage built in 1935 in Cross Lane. The old building was converted into flats known as Beech Hall, but in 1939-40 it underwent a further change of use, becoming Grove Park School for boys. It was demolished in 1983 and replaced by eight houses called Beechill.

Ottershaw Junior School c. 1910

The Church of England or National School opened in 1870 was also built through the generosity of Sir Edward Colebrooke. Originally built to house 120 pupils in separate junior and infants' departments, the school also received children from the Workhouse, and after 1885 from the Meath Homes in Brox Road. The increasing school roll was eased in 1906 when the infant department moved to the new school in Brox Road. At the time when the photograph was taken, Henry Baker was Headmaster and the average attendance was 147. The school building was closed in 1967 and converted during 1985 into seven individual mews cottages known as Colebrooke Place.

Durnford Lodge c. 1908

Craftsmen and labourers pose outside the new house they have just completed – Durnford Lodge, soon to be occupied by Charles Taylor, who was Bailiff at Ottershaw Park. He remained in residence until 1941, when the lease was taken over by the Government for the duration of the War.

The Castle, Brox, c. 1905

The Castle was built in 1840 and operated as a beerhouse by William and Mary Gifkins, who were also running the adjacent nursery. Charles Brookson, landlord at the time of this photograph, added the extension seen on the left in 1905. He too was working as a nurseryman in addition to running the pub, and held the licence until his death aged 75 in January 1929, after 31 years in Ottershaw.

Brox Road c. 1930

Seen here looking north from near the corner of Southwood Avenue, Brox Road, widened in 1927, seems a quiet road. The houses on the left now have extensions and other alterations, while many of the gaps between have been filled with newer homes.

Bousley Rise c. 1950

Bousley Rise was no more than a track to Bousley Farm until housing development at its eastern end began in the 1920s. The farm, like much of the surrounding area, was operated as a nursery in the 19th century, but it was sold c. 1925 to Mr. Edward Burree. He used the farm for market gardening, and this view, probably taken in June, shows a crop of cauliflowers in the foreground, soon to be packed into the collapsible wooden crates beside the track. Stacks of empty market boxes and a trailer wait near the building behind, and beyond that in neat rows can be seen stacks of Dutch lights used for growing carrots, turnips and marrows. Mr. Burree's son Arthur eventually sold the farm in 1950 to Mr. A. Van den Broek, and it reverted to its former use as a nursery.

Slade Road, 1930s

In 1920 Slade Road was little more than a country lane, with just a handful of dwellings about halfway along, and was known as "The Slade", a local dialect word meaning a small valley. This view from the south-western end, taken in the 1930s, still shows a quiet, though more populated road, and by this time the present street name had come into use.

Infants' School, Brox Road, c. 1910

The schools in Guildford Road having become overcrowded, Lady Meath gave Ottershaw a new infants' school in Brox Road, built in 1905 and opened the following year. The Editor of the Parish Magazine had commented: "It is furnished in good style, convenient, and the best appointed in Surrey.", but the amount of traffic in Brox Road had occasioned great concern in the parish. It was designed to accommodate 80 children, but at this time the average attendance was 55. The mistress until the mid-1920s was Miss Rose Busby, who can be seen here supervising the children in the grassed playground. The boys, wearing the sailor suits so popular at this time, seem reluctant to join the girls playing "ring-a-ring-o'-roses" or similar games. The school closed in 1967 when the new First School opened, and the building was converted into a restaurant.

Brox Road, Ottershaw, c. 1932

Around 1912, Ottershaw Post Office had moved to its present site in Brox Road and was then run by Charles Goldring, together with a bakery. At the time this photograph was taken John Sylvester Chance was in occupation and was also a baker. The building then housed Ottershaw's telephone exchange and had telephone number 1. On its wall, the sign stating "Established 1851" seems to refer to the previous Post Office Stores opposite The Otter in Guildford Road.

Chertsey Union House, 1st January 1917

Chertsey's original "House of Maintenance" was situated on the site of the present Chertsey Station by 1726. Under the Poor Law Amendment Act of 1834, parishes were grouped into "Unions" which encouraged the building of new and larger buildings to house the poor and indigent. The Chertsey Poor Law Institution was opened in 1837 and closed in 1930. Pictured here are some of the elderly inmates of the time being visited by Mr. Driver of Horsell, whose pack of hounds were kennelled at Homestead Farm, Longcross. This New Year's Day event seems to have been something of an annual ritual, and on this occasion no fewer than five London press photographers were on hand to record the scene. As well as gifts of sweets for the women, there was tobacco for the men and toys for the children who also lived here. Even the Workhouse had not escaped the effects of the First World War, as from 1915 the Ottershaw building also housed inmates from the Guildford and Richmond Institutions, theirs having been taken over for War Hospitals. Among the residents at the time were a man of 96 and a woman of 94. In 1930 it was renamed Murray House and converted to house the mentally handicapped.

Steam Ploughing at Great Grove Farm c. 1910

Part of the Botleys Park Estate owned by Herbert Gosling, the farm was tenanted at this time by Thomas Minshall, a civil engineer. The heavy clay soil of the area was ideally suited to steam ploughing: a technique for drawing a plough with steel cables between two stationary engines. These machines were operated by the major local agricultural contractors, A.J. Ward of Thorpe Lea, Egham. Built by Fowler's, their single cylinders with Church valve gear produced 12 h.p.